MOHAVE TRIBE

by
Mary Null Boulé

Illustrated by
Daniel Liddell

Merryant Publishers, Inc.
Vashon, WA 98070
206-463-3879

This series is dedicated to Virginia Harding, whose editing, expertise and friendship brought this project to fruition.

See map enclosed for position of Mohave tribe.

ISBN #1-877599-57-3

Copyright © 2000, Merryant Publishing

7615 S.W. 257th St., Vashon, WA 98070.

FOREWORD

Native American people of the United States are often living their lives away from major cities and away from what we call the mainstream of life. It is, then, interesting to learn of the important part these remote tribal members play in our everyday lives.

More than 60% of our foods come from the ancient Native American's diet. Farming methods of today also can be traced back to how tribal women grew crops of corn and grain. Many of our present-day ideas of democracy have been taken from tribal governments. Even some 1,500 Native American words are found in our English language today.

Fur traders bought furs from tribal hunters for small amounts of money, sold them to Europeans and Asians for a great deal of money, and became rich. Using their money to buy land and to build office buildings, some traders started business corporations which are now the base of our country's economy.

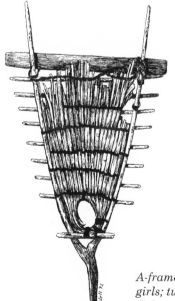

There has never been enough credit given to these early Americans who took such good care of our country when it was still in their care. The time has come to realize tribal contributions to our society today and to give Native Americans not only the credit, but the respect due them.

Mary Boulé

A-frame cradle for girls; tule matting. Tubatulabal tribe.

GENERAL INFORMATION

Creation legends told by today's tribal people speak of how, very long ago, their creator placed them in a territory, where they became caretakers of that land and its animals. None of their ancient legends tells about the first Native Americans coming from another continent.

It is important to respect the different beliefs and theories, to learn from and seek the truth in all of them.

Villagers' tribal history lessons do not agree with the beliefs of anthropologists (scientific historians who study the habits and customs of humans).

Clues found by these scientists lead them to believe that ancient tribespeople came to North America from Asia during the Ice Age period some 20 to 35 thousand years ago. They feel these humans walked over a land strip in the Bering Straits, following animal herds who provided them with food.

Scientists' understanding of ancient people must come from studying clues; for example, tools, utensils, baskets, garbage discoveries, and stories they passed from one generation to the next.

California's Native Americans did not organize into large tribes. Instead they divided into tribelets, sometimes having as many as 250 people. Some tribelets had only one chief for each village.

From 20 to 100 people could be living in one village, which usually had several houses. In most cases, these groups of people were one family and were related to each other. From five to ten people of a family might live in one house. For instance, a mother, a father, two or three children, a grandmother, or aunt or daughter-in-law might live together.

Village members together would own the land important to them for their well-being. Their land might include oak trees with precious acorns, streams and rivers, and plants which were good to eat. Streams and rivers were especially important to a tribe's quality of life. Water drew animals to it; that meant more food for the tribe to eat. Fish were a good source of food, and traveling by boat was often easier than walking long distances. Water was needed in every part of tribal life.

Village and tribelet land was carefully guarded. Each group knew exactly where the boundaries of its land were found. Boundaries were known by landmarks such as mountains or rivers, or they might also be marked by poles planted in the ground. Some boundary lines were marked by rocks, or by objects placed there by tribal members. The size of a territory had to be large enough to supply food to every person living there.

The California tribes spoke many languages. sometimes villages close together even had a problem understanding one another. This meant that each group had to be sure of the boundaries of other tribes around them when gathering food. It would not be wise to go against the boundaries and the customs of neighbors. The Native Americans found if they respected the boundaries of their neighbors, not so many wars had to be fought. California tribes, in spite of all their differences, were not as warlike as other tribes in our country.

Not only did the California tribes speak different languages, but their members also differed in size. Some tribes were very tall, almost six feet tall. The shortest people came from the Yuki tribe which had territory in what is now Mendocino County. They measured only about 5'2" tall. All Native Americans, regardless of size, had strong, straight black hair and dark brown eyes.

TRADE

Trading between tribes was an important part of life. Inland tribes had large animal hides that coastal tribes wanted. By trading the hides to coastal groups, inland tribes would receive fish and shells, which they in turn wanted. Coastal tribes also wanted minerals and rocks mined in the mountains by inland tribes. Obisdian rock from the northern mountains was especially wanted for arrowheads. There were, as well, several minerals, mined in the inland mountains, which could be made into the colorful body paints needed for religious ceremonies.

Southern tribes particularly wanted steatite from the Gabrielino tribe. Steatite, or soapstone, was a special metal which allowed heat to spread evenly through it. This made it a good choice to be used for cooking pots and flat frying pans. It could be carved into bowls because of its softness and could be decorated by carving designs into it. Steatite came from Catalina Island in the Coastal Gabrielino territory. Gabrielinos found steatite to be a fine trading item to offer for the acorns, deerskins, or obsidian stone they needed.

When people had no items to trade but needed something, they used small strings of shells for money. The small dentalium shells, which came from the far distant Northwest coast, had great value. Strings of dentalia usually served as money in the Northern California tribes, although some dentalia was used in the Central California tribes.

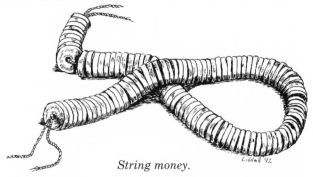

String money.

6

In southern California clam shells were broken and holes were bored through the center of each piece. Then the pieces were rounded and polished with sandstone and strung into strings for money. These were not thought to be as valuable as dentalia.

Strings of shell money were measured by tattoo marks on the trader's lower arm or hand.

Here is a sample of shell value:

A house, three strings
A fishing place, one to three strings
Land with acorn-bearing oak trees, one to five strings

A great deal of rock and stone was traded among the tribes for making tools. Arrows had to have sharp-edged stone for tips. The best stone for arrow tips was obsidian (volcanic glass) because, when hit properly, it broke off into flakes with very sharp edges. California tribes considered obsidian to be the most valuable rock for trading.

Some tribes had craftsmen who made knives with wooden handles and obsidian blades. Often the handles were decorated with carvings. Such knives were good for trading purposes. Stone mortars and pestles, used by the women for grinding grains into flour, were good trading items.

BASKETS & POTTERY

California tribal women made beautiful baskets. The Pomo and Chumash baskets, what few are left, show us that the women of those tribes might have been some of the finest basketmakers in the world. Baskets were used for gathering and storing food, for carrying babies, and even for hauling water. In emergencies, such as flooding waters, sometimes children, women, and tribal belongings crossed the swollen rivers and streams in huge, woven baskets! Baskets were so tightly woven that not a drop of water could leak from them.

Baskets also made fine cooking pots. Very hot rocks were taken from a fire and tossed around inside baskets with a looped tree branch until food in the basket was cooked.

Most baskets were made to do a certain job, but some baskets were designed for their beauty alone and were excellent for trading. Older women of a tribe would teach young girls how to weave baskets.

California hunter wearing deerskin camoflage.

Pottery was not used by many California tribes. What little there was seems to have been made by those tribes living near to the Navaho and Mohave tribes of Arizona, and it shows their style. For example, pottery of the California tribes did not have much decoration and was usually a dull red color. Designs were few and always in yellow.

Long thin coils of clay were laid one on top the other. Then

the coils were smoothed between a wooden paddle and a small stone to shape the bowl. Pottery from California Native Americans has been described as light weight and brittle (easily broken), probably because of the kind of clay soil found in California.

HUNTING & FISHING

Tribal men spent much of their time making hunting and fishing tools. Bows and arrows were built with great care, to make them shoot as accurately as possible. Carelessly made hunting weapons caused fewer animals to be killed and people then had less food to eat.

Bows made by men of Southern California tribes were made long and narrow. In the northern part of the state bows were a little shorter, thinner, and wider than those of their northern neighbors. Size and thickness of bows depended on the size trees growing in a tribe's territory. The strongest bows were wrapped with sinew, the name given to animal tendons. Sinew is strong and elastic like a rubber band.

Arrows were made in many sizes and shapes, depending on their use. For hunting larger animals, a two-piece arrow was used. The front piece of the arrow shaft was made so that it would remain in the animal, even if the back part was removed or broken off. The arrowhead, or point, was wrapped to the front piece of the shaft. This kind of arrow was also used in wars.

Young boys used a simple wooden arrow with the end sharpened to a point. With this they could hunt small animals like birds and rabbits. The older men of the tribe taught boys how to make their own arrows, how to aim properly, and how to repair broken weapons.

Tribal men spent many hours making and mending fishing nets. The string used in making nets often came from the fibers of plants. These fibers were twisted to make them strong and tough, then knotted into netting. Fences, or weirs, that had one small opening for fish, were built across streams. As the fish swam through the opening they would be caught in netting or harpooned by a waiting fisherman.

Hooks, if used at all, were cut from shells. Mostly hooks could be found when the men fished in large lakes or when catching trout in high mountain areas. Hooks were attached to heavy plant fiber string.

Dip nets, made of netting attached to branches that were bent into a circle, were used to catch fish swimming near shore. Dip nets had long handles so the fishermen could reach deep into the water.

Sometimes a mild poison was placed on the surface of shallow water. This confused the fish and caused them to float to the surface of the water, where they could be scooped up by a waiting fisherman. Not enough poison was used to make humans ill.

Not all fishing was done from the shore. California tribes used two kinds of boats when fishing. Canoes, dug out of one half a log, were useful for river fishing. These were square at each end, round on the bottom, and very heavy. Some of them were well-finished, often even having a carved seat in them.

Today we think of "balsa" as a very lightweight wood, but in Spanish, the word balsa means "raft". That is why Spanish explorers called the Native American canoes, made from tule reeds, "balsa" boats.

Balsa boats were made of bundled tule reeds and were used throughout most of California. They made into safe, lightweight boats for lake and river use. Usually the balsa canoe had a long, tightly tied bundle of tule for the boat bottom and one bundle for each side of the canoe. The front of the canoe was higher than the back. Balsa boats could be steered with a pole or with a paddle, like a raft.

Men did most of the fishing, women were in charge of gathering grasses, seeds, and acorns for food. After the food was collected, it was either eaten right away or made ready for winter storage.

Except for a few southern groups, California tribes had permanent villages where they lived most of the year. They also had food-gathering places they returned to each year to collect acorns, salt, fish, and other foods not found near their villages.

FOOD

Many different kinds of plant food grew wild in California in the days before white people arrived. Berries and other plant foods grew in the mountains. Forests offered the local tribes everything from pine nuts to animals.

Native Americans found streams full of fish for much of the year. Inland fresh water lakes had large tule reeds growing along their shores. Tule could be eaten as food when plants were young and tender. More important, however, tule was used in making fabric for clothes and for building boats and houses. Tule was probably the most useful plant the California Native Americans found growing wild in their land.

Like all deserts, the one in southern California had little water or fish, but small animals and cactus plants made good food for the local tribes. They moved from place to place harvesting whatever was ripe. Tribal members always knew when and where to find the best food in their territory.

Acorns were the main source of food for all California tribes. Acorn flour was as important to the California Native Americans as wheat is to us today. Five types of California oak trees produced acorns that could be eaten. Those from black oak and tanbark oak seem to have been the favorite kinds.

Since some acorns tasted better than others, the tastiest ones were collected first. If harvest of the favorite acorn was poor some years, then less tasty acorns had to be eaten all winter long.

So important were acorns to California Indians that most tribes built their entire year around them. Acorn harvest marked the beginning of their calendar year. Winter was counted as so many months after acorn harvest, and summer was counted by the number of months before the next acorn harvest.

Acorn harvest ceremonies usually were the biggest events of the year. Most celebrations took place in mid-October and included dancing, feasts, games of chance, and reunions with relatives. Harvest festivals lasted for many days. They were a time of joy for everyone.

The annual acorn gathering lasted two to three weeks. Young boys climbed the oak trees to shake branches; some men used long poles to knock acorns to the ground. Women loaded the nuts into large cone-shaped burden baskets and carried them to a central place where they were put in the sun to dry.

Once the acorns were dried, the women carried them back to the tribe's permanent villages. There they lined special basket-like storage granaries with strong herbs to keep insects away, then stored the acorns inside. Granaries were placed on stilts to keep animals from getting into them and were kept beside tribal houses.

Preparing acorns for each meal was also the women's job. Shells were peeled by hitting the acorns with a stone hammer on an anvil (flat) stone. Meat from the nut was then laid on a stone mortar. A mortar was usually a large stone with a slight dip on its surface. Sometimes the mortar had a bottomless basket, called a hopper, glued to its top. This kept the acorn meat from sliding off the mortar as it was beaten. The meat was then pounded with a long stone pestle. Acorn flour was scraped away from the hopper's sides with a soaproot fiber brush during this process.

From there the flour was put into an open-worked basket and sifted. A fine flour came through the bottom of the basket, while the larger pieces were put back in the mortar for more pounding.

The most important process came after the acorn flour was sifted. Acorn flour has a very bitter-tasting tannin in it. This bitter taste was removed by a method called leaching. Many tribes leached the flour by first scooping out a hollow in sand near water. The hollow was lined with leaves to keep the flour from washing away. A great deal of hot water was poured through the flour to wash out (leach) the bitterness. Sometimes the flour was put into a basket for the leaching process, instead of using sand and leaves.

Finally the acorn flour was ready to be cooked. To make mush, heated stones were placed in the basket with the flour. A looped tree branch or two long sticks were used to toss the hot rocks around so the basket would not burn. When the mush had boiled, it could be eaten. If the flour and water mixture was baked in an earthen oven, it became a kind of bread. Early explorers wrote that it was very tasty.

Historians have estimated that one family would eat from 1500 to 2000 pounds of acorn flour a year. One reason California native Americans did not have to plant seeds and raise crops was because there were so many acorns for them to harvest each year.

Whether they ate fish or shellfish or plant food or animal meat, nature supplied more than enough food for the Native Americans who lived in California long ago. Many believed their good fortune in having fine weather and plenty to eat came from being good to their gods.

RELIGION

Tribal members had strong beliefs in the power of spirits or gods around them. Each tribe was different, but all felt the importance of never making a spirit angry with them. For that reason a celebration to thank the spirit-gods for treating them well, took place before each food gathering and before each hunting trip, and after each food harvest.

Usually spiritual powers were thought to belong to birds or animals. Most California tribespeople felt bears were very wicked and should not be eaten. But Coyote seems to have been a kind leader who helped them if they were in trouble, even though he seems to have been a bit naughty at times. Eagle was thought to be very powerful and good to native Americans. In some tribes, Eagle was almost as powerful as Sun.

Tribes placed importance on different gods, according to the tribe's needs. Rain gods were the most important spirits to desert tribes. Weather gods, who might bring less rain or warmer temperatures, were important to northern tribes. A great many groups felt there were gods for each of the winds: North, South, East and West. The four directions were usually included in their ceremonial dances and

Religious feather charm.

were used as part of the decorations on baskets, pots, and even tools.

Animals were not only worshipped and believed to be spirit-gods, like Deer or Antelope, but tribal members felt there was a personal animal guardian for each one of them. If a tribal member had a deer as guardian, then that person could never kill a deer or eat deer meat.

California Native Americans believed in life after death. This made them very respectful of death and very fearful of angering a dead person. Once someone died, the name of the dead person could never again be said aloud. Since it was easy to accidentally say a name aloud, the name was usually given to a new baby. Then the dead person would not become angry.

Shamans were thought to be the keepers of religious beliefs and to have the ability to talk directly to spirit-gods. It was the job of a village shaman to cure sick people, and to speak to the gods about the needs of the people. Some tribes had several kinds of shamans in one village. One shaman did curing, one scared off evil spirits, while another took care of hunters.

Not all shamans were nice, so people greatly feared their power. However, if shamans had no luck curing sick people or did not bring good luck in hunting, the people could kill them. Most shamans were men, but in a few tribes, women were doctors.

Most California tribal myths have been lost to history because they were spoken and never written down. The legends were told and retold on winter nights around the home fires. Sadly, these were forgotten after the missionaries brought Christianity to California and moved tribal members into the missions.

A few stories still remain, however. It is thought by historians that northwest California tribes were the only ones not to have a myth on how they were created. They did not feel that the world was made and prepared for human beings. Instead, their few remaining stories usually tell of mountain peaks or rivers in their own territory.

The central California tribes had creation stories of a great flood where there was only water on earth. They tell of how man was made from a bit of mud that a turtle brought up from the bottom of the water.

Many southwest tribes believed there was a time of no sky or water. They told of two clouds appearing which finally became Sky and Earth.

Throughout California, however, all tribes had myths that told of Eagle as the leader, Coyote as chief assistant, and of less powerful spirits like Falcon or Hawk.

Costumes for religious ceremonies often imitated these animals they worshipped or feared. Much time was spent in making the dance costumes as beautiful as possible. Red woodpecker feathers were so brilliant a color they were used to decorate religious headdresses, necklaces, or belts. Deerskin clothing was fringed so shell beads could be attached to each thin strip of leather.

Eagle feathers were felt to be the most sacred of religious objects. Sometimes they were made into whole robes. Usually, though, the feathers were used just for decorations. All these costumes were valuable to the people of each tribe. The village chief was in charge of taking care of the costumes, and there was terrible punishment for stealing them. Clothing worn everyday was not fancy like costuming for rituals.

CLOTHING

Central and southern California's fine weather made regular clothes not really very important to the Native Americans. The children and men went naked most of the year, but most women wore a short apron-like skirt. These skirts

Willow bark skirt.

were usually made in two pieces, front and back aprons, with fringes cut into the bottom edges. Often the skirt was made from the inner bark of trees, shredded and gathered on a cord. Sometimes the skirt was made from tule or grass.

In northern California and in rainy or windy weather elsewhere in the state, animal-skin blankets were worn by both men and women. They were used like a cape and wrapped around the body. Sometimes the cape was put over one shoulder and under the other arm, then tied in front. All kinds of skins were used; deer, otter, wildcat, but sea-otter fur was thought to be the best. If the skin was from a small animal, it was cut into strips and woven together into a fabric. At night the cape became a blanket to keep the person warm.

Because of the rainy weather in northern California, the women wore basket caps all the time. Women of the central and south tribes wore caps only when carrying heavy loads, where the forehead had to be used as support. Then a cap helped keep too much weight from being placed on the forehead.

Most California people went barefoot in their villages. For journeys into rough land, going to war, wood gathering, or in colder weather, the tribesmen in central and north-west California wore a one-piece soft shoe with no extra sole, which went high up on the leg.

Southern California tribespeople, however, wore sandals most of the time, wearing high, soled moccasins only when they traveled long distances or into the mountains. Leggings of skin were worn in snow, and moccasins were sometimes lined with grass for more comfort and warmth.

VILLAGE LIFE

Houses of the California tribes were made of materials found in their area. Usually they were round with domed roofs. Except for a few tribes, a house floor was dug into the earth a few feet. This was wise, for it made the home warmer in winter and cooler in summer. It also meant that less material was needed to make house walls.

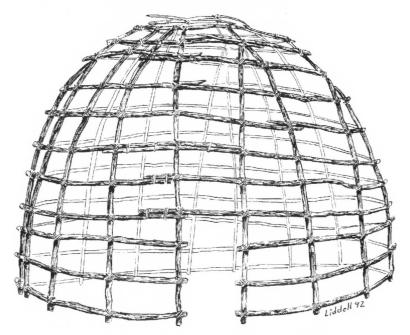

Framework of house – bundles of grass were laid over the framework.

Framework for the walls was made from bendable branches tied to support poles. Some frames of the houses were covered with earth and grass. Others were covered with large slabs of redwood or pine bark. Central California villagers made large woven mats of tule reed to cover the tops and sides of houses. In the warmer southern area, brush and smaller pieces of bark were used for house walls.

Most California Native American villages had a building called a sweathouse, where the men could be found when they were not hunting, fishing or traveling. It was a very important place for the men, who used it rather like a clubhouse. They could sweat and then scrape themselves clean with curved ribs of deer. The sweathouse was smaller than a family house. Normally it had a center pole framework with a firepit on the ground next to the pole. When the fire was lit, some smoke was allowed to escape through a hole at the top of the roof; however, most was trapped inside the building. Smoke and heat were the main reasons for having a sweathouse. Both were believed to be a way to purify tribal members' bodies. Sweathouse walls were mainly hard-packed earth. The heat produced was not a steam heat but came from a wood-fed fire.

In the center of most villages was a large house that often had no walls, just a roof held up with poles. It was here that religious dances and rituals were held, or visitors were entertained.

Dances were enjoyed and were performed with great skill. Music, usually only rhythm instruments, accompanied the dances. For some reason California Native Americans did not use drums to create rhythms for their dances. Three different kinds of rattles were used by California tribes.

One type, split-clap sticks, created rhythm for dancing. These were usually a length of cane (a hollow stick) split in half lengthwise for about two-thirds of its length. The part still uncut was tightly wound with cord so it would not split

Split-stick clapper, rhythm instrument, Hupa tribe.

all the way. The stick was held at the tied end in one hand and hit against the palm of the other hand to make its sound.

A pebble-filled moth cocoon made rhythm for shaman duties. These could range from calling on spirits to cure illnesses, to performing dances to bring rain. Probably the best sounds to beat rhythm for songs and dances came from bundles of deer hooves tied together on a stick. These rattles have a hollow, warm sound.

The only really "musical" instrument found in California was a flute made of reed that was played by blowing across the edge of one end. Melodies were not played on any of these instruments. Most North American Indians sang their songs rather than playing melodies on music instruments.

Special songs were sung for each event. There were songs for healing sick people, songs for success in hunting, war, or marriage. Women sang acorn-grinding songs and lullabies. Songs were sung in sorrow for the dead and during story-telling times. Group singing, with a leader, was the favorite kind of singing. Most songs were sung by all tribe members, but religious songs had to be sung by a special group. It was important that sacred songs not be changed through the years. If a mistake was made while singing sacred music, the singer could be punished, so only specially trained singers would sing ritual songs.

All songs were very short, some of them only 20 to 30 seconds long. They were made longer by repeating the melodies over and over, or by connecting several songs together. Songs usually told no story, just repeated words or phrases or syllables in patterns.

Song melodies used only one or two notes and harmony was never added. Perhaps that is why mission Indians, at those missions with musician priests, especially loved to sing harmony in the church choirs.

Songs and dances were good methods of passing rich tribal traditions on to the children. It was important to tribal adults that their children understand and love the tribe's heritage.

Children were truly wanted by parents in most tribes and new parents carefully watched their tiny babies day and night, to be sure they stayed warm and dry. Usually a newborn was strapped into a cradle and tied to the mother's back so she could continue to work, yet be near the baby at all times. In some tribes, older children took care of babies of cradle age during the day to give the mother time to do all her work, while grandmothers were often in charge of caring for toddlers.

Children were taught good behavior, traditions, and tribal rules from babyhood, although some tribes were stricter than others. Most of the time parents made their children obey. Young children could be lightly punished, but in many tribes those over six or seven years old were more severely punished if they did not follow the rules.

Just as children do today, Native American youngsters had childhood traditions they followed. For instance, one tribal tradition said that when a baby tooth came out, a child waited until dusk, faced the setting sun and threw the tooth to the west. There is no mention of a generous tooth fairy, however.

Tribal parents were worried that their offspring might not be strong and brave. Some tribes felt one way to make their children stronger was by forcing them to bathe in ice cold water, even in wintertime. Every once in a while, for example, Modoc children were awakened from sleep and taken to a cold lake or stream for a freezing bath.

But if freezing baths at night were hard on young Native Americans, their days were carefree and happy. Children were allowed to play all day, and some tribes felt children did not even have to come to dinner if they didn't want to. In those tribes, children could come to their houses to eat anytime of the day.

The games boys played are not too different from those played today. Swimming, hide and seek among the tule reeds, a form of tetherball with a mud ball tied to a pole, and willow-javelin throwing kept boys busy throughout the day.

Fathers made their sons small bows and arrows, so boys spent much time trying to improve their hunting skills. They practised shooting at frogs or chipmunks. The first animal any boy killed was not touched or eaten by him. Others would carry the kill home to be cooked and eaten by villagers. This tradition taught boys always to share food.

Another hunting tool for boys was a hollowed-out willow branch. This became like a modern day beanshooter, only the Native American boys shot juniper berries instead of beans. Slingshots made good hunting weapons, as well.

Girls and boys shared many games, but girls playing with each other had contests to see who could make a basket the fastest, or they played with dolls made of tule. Together, young boys and girls played a type of ring-around-the-rosie game, climbed mountains, or built mud houses.

As children grew older, the boys followed their fathers and the girls followed their mothers as the adults did their daily work. Children were not trained in the arts of hunting or basketmaking, however, until they became teenagers.

HISTORY

Spanish missionaries, led by Fray Junipero Serra, arrived in California in 1769 to build missions along the coast of California. By 1823, fifty-four years later, 21 missions had been founded. Almost all of them were very successful, and the Franciscan monks who ran them were proud of how many Native Americans became Christians.

However, all was not as the monks had planned it would be. Native American people had never been around the diseases European white men brought with them. As a result, they had no immunity to such illnesses as measles, small pox, or flu. Too many mission Indians died from white men's diseases.

Historians figure there were 300,000 Native Americans living in California before the missionaries came. The missions show records of 83,000 mission Indians during mission days. By the time the Mexicans took over the missions from the Spanish in 1834, only 20,000 remained alive.

The great California Gold Rush of 1849 was probably another big reason why many of the Native Americans died during that time. White men, staking their claim to tribal lands with gold upon it, thought nothing of killing any California tribesman who tried to keep and protect his territory. Fifty-thousand tribal members died from diseases, bullets, or starvation between the gold Rush Days and 1870. By 1910, only 17,000 California Indians remained.

Although the American government tried to set aside reservations (areas reserved for Native Americans), the land given to the Indians often was not good land. Worse yet, some of the land sacred to tribes, such as burial grounds, was taken over by white people and never given back.

Sadly, mission Indians, when they became Christians, forgot the proud heritage and beliefs they had followed for thousands of years. Many wonderful myths and songs they had passed from one generation to the next, on winter nights so long ago, have been lost forever.

Today some 100,000 people can claim California Native American ancestors, but few pure-blooded tribespeople remain. Our link with the Wanderers, who came from Asia so long ago, has been forever broken.

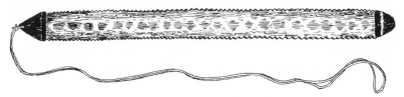

The bullroarer made a deep, loud sound when whirled above the player's head. Tipai tribe.

Villages were usually built beside a lake, stream, or river. Balsa canoes are on the shore. Tule reeds grow along the edge of the water and are drying on poles on the right side of the picture.

Women preparing food in baskets, sit on tule mats. Tule mats are being tied to the willow pole framework of a house being built by one of the men.

MOHAVE PEOPLE

INTRODUCTION

Historians think the word Mohave (Mo' hahv ee) came from the Spanish word, hamakhav, which the tribe gave to itself. The name probably means "people who live along the water," because the Mohave natives lived as they still do now, mostly on the western desert shore of the Colorado River. Since this was desert, there was very little water on their land, so the river meant life to them, when it flooded each spring.

Before white people came, the three ancient Mohave groups were one tribe, often coming together for wars. The full tribe's ancient population may have reached 20,000 people.

Scientists who research ancient humans seem to think these people were among the tallest people on our whole North American continent. Research tells us they had broad heavy-looking faces, skin of a dark, nut-like color, brown eyes, and straight black hair.

Although these are all Mohave women, the men also wore long hair.

Many scientists feel the Mohave natives were quite emotional. For example, at funerals they easily showed their sadness by crying loudly. At all kinds of events, good or bad, happy or sad, Mohave people seemed to freely show how they felt.

These natives were very curious about other people and loved to travel to see how others lived. They were eager to know the manners of those tribes around them, so they would make sure they NEVER did those things themselves!

In their everyday lives, Mohave people were warriors, fishermen, and farmers, who grew over 50% of their food. In fact, although they were mainly farmers and fishermen, war seems to have been almost the most important thing in young men's lives. Studies show there was a group of 40—50 men for whom war was their only thought. As a result, group leaders would often take men to fight natives around them. This band of natives had more than three times as many wars as any other group in their area.

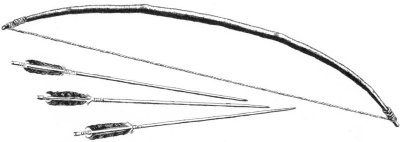

Mohave bows were not wrapped for strength and were about six feet long. Arrows were shorter.

Ordinarily, men divided into two groups for a war; one group had bows five feet long and quivers full of long-distance arrows for fighting; another group fought enemies with clubs and heavy sticks. Most of these young warriors held round animalskin (hide) shields against their bodies for protection. Many of the fights were about territory.

Mohave people, rather than having usual villages of families, were scattered in settlements, or bands, throughout their territory. But in pre-explorer times it was most heavily populated in a place known today as the Mohave Valley.

Some scientists feel the Mohave people might have settled on the Colorado River bank as early as a.d. (after Christ's birth) 1150 years ago.

TERRITORY, VILLAGE SITES, HOMES

The ancient Mohave territory was divided into three band areas for their tribal members. One band lay in the northern part of the land, one in the southern region, and one lay in the center between the north and south. People moved freely among the three regions.

In ancient days, Mohave natives were found on either side of the Colorado River in what has since become the states of California and Arizona. The bands lived along the Colorado River from 15 miles north of the present-day Davis dam, south for 170 river miles, almost to today's city of Blythe, California.

One researcher said the Mohave people were found in "Rancherias" made up of two or three houses along the Colorado River. Boundaries of growing fields were marked by ridges of dirt or with boundary markers put up along the edges. It was when flooding changed the markers that wars might begin among the natives.

This was a region of mild winters, very hot, dry summers, and almost no rain. The huge Colorado River was the only large body of water found in this part of what is now California. There were a few water holes for desert territory, which Native Americans could share.

Water could be carried in a gourd, so water did not seep through.

Most of the year, the rainless desert had few plants. Cactus plants and creosote bushes grew naturally. But once a year at springtime, Rocky Mountain snow thawed and swelled the Colorado River. The river flooded and covered about one mile of land between the river and mountains with rich and damp soil, just right for growing food. This created a long, narrow strip of green through the desert.

The yearly flooding made it possible for people and animals to live there; by giving rich soil, it gave Mohaves half of their food needs. Because of the flood waters, dense cane, arrowweed, and groves of cottonwood and willows also grew wild there.

Families usually always had some kind of food, as few people lived in the hot desert, itself. However, when food was low, the Mohave people found they had to hunt, gather, fish. They would collect piñon nuts from pine trees, mesquite beans, and even eat insects.

Natives built homes overlooking the fields planted with corn, beans, pumpkins, and melons. Their springtime settlements were more like farms than villages and were often five miles from each other. Winter homes were from one to two miles apart. These were low, rectangular, built of insulated thatch walls from thick river mud and covered with sand roofs that were sloped on the sides and ends.

An ancient house, still in use in the mid 1800s, did not often have doors, but walls built of long arrowwood branches piled behind the wall supports. Doors came later, for privacy.

Cottonwood-tree posts formed building frameworks. Thick front walls were layered with tall, stacked, arrowwood branches, which grew wild along the river. These branches were packed behind eight-foot-tall-logs. This kind of wall protected the people from the cooler weather and made the houses almost invisible to trespassers.

There were still homes like this until the late 1800s. The sand-covered roofs with their raised edges were used for storage as well as big meeting places for village men.

Long ago there were some winter homes that were placed beside each other in a long C shape. These homes were about 20-25 feet wide and faced south, with the front wall left open to the outside. Later, doors also were added for privacy. This kind of home had stout centerposts and a ridgepole with rafters. The outer walls of the home were made of long branches of arrowweed tightly packed together between wall support poles.

During most of the year however, Mohave people were able to live under flat-topped, ramadas (meaning "shade" in Spanish) which had no walls.

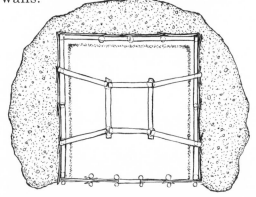

Diagram of Mohave house, first from above the house and then from the front.

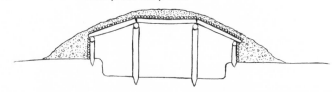

VILLAGE LIFE

As stated before, the lives of the Mohave people centered around the Colorado River, which flowed through their daily lives. They swam the river, pushing a log ahead of them which carried food in large pots; sometimes even swimming and pushing small children in the large pots. Rafts were used to carry belongings across the river when they went on long trips.

There was one head chief, plus subchiefs, leading each of the three smaller bands. Actually, the whole group did not have much real organization. For instance, there was no main tribal council; however, a chief might sometimes meet with important people, who then spoke to the natives in the mornings from a house rooftop. Chiefs, in most cases, had little power, but were more into how people acted.

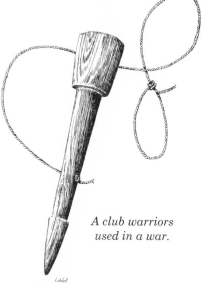

A club warriors used in a war.

Some Mohaves were thought to be fine, skillful speakers. Being good speakers meant these people could be made into leaders of their tribe. They were felt to have power through dreams. Plain dreams would be used as omens for such activities as war against old enemies, mainly the Maricopas or the Cocopahs of Arizona.

Women were called by their families' names. These names could come from those given to plants growing around them or from those of animals found in their territory; names such as maize (corn) or gourd.

Marriage was usually an event with no ceremony or rules. What's more, marriages were often arranged by families, without the couples themselves even being in on the choosing of mates. Couples simply began living together. There were not even rules about where a new couple would live.

Mohaves had few public ceremonies and almost no dancing. As a result, there were no masks or religious objects used, just the singing of about 30 song cycles. These song cycles took all night to perform. Rhythm was kept with gourd rattles or the beating on an overturned basket, rather than a drum, or using just a stick.

For entertainment, villagers loved to play a game called shinney, which had to do with batting a small block of wood with a curved stick.

LIFE CYCLE

There also were no rituals when a baby was born. Usually parents were always supposed to be happy at all times around a baby, so as not to make their child hard to handle.

Children's toy.

Child-raising was based on not punishing them very often. Most of the time children just played. When they were being educated in grown-up ways of life, there still was little pressure on them, since it was believed they were being taught by dreams. Even though teen-agers might be trained by their dreams, they learned from their families how to grow and gather food.

When natives became ill, the family shaman was called to use his/her power to help the sick person. If a native was dying, friends and relatives came to visit. They would sing and wail, trying to help the sick person.

Children's toy.

As soon as possible after death, a body was cremated (burned) with all his or her belongings. Funeral orators, or speakers, made speeches telling of the good ways of a dead person. Two hundred songs were sung in thirty cycles. Mourners wailed their songs faster and faster when the fire was lit. These songs would last all night.

Natives who sang felt that by burning all belongings owned by a dead native, these things would be sent with the body's soul. Even stored grains found in the dead person's granary were burned. Mohave belief was that the ghost of a dead native stayed around the cremation fire for four days, to revisit all the events of its life.

After four days, Mohaves thought a body went to the Land of the Dead. It was believed The Land of the Dead was in sand hills in the southern part of the Mohave Valley, near the Needles Peaks. This place was thought to be pleasant, and a place where other dead people welcomed them. It was also a place of no pain or sickness and always had good food. Mohave people felt a soul did not live forever, but finally became charcoal on the surrounding desert.

RELIGION

It is believed by Mohave people that Motovilya was the tribe's hero. Their creation story tells of the day there was a bonding of Earth and Sky, that became the world of land around the Colorado River. All villagers believed (as they still do today), that in the beginning natives had been placed on their territory by the Creator. Mohaves today also still believe that Spirit Mountain in their territory is especially holy.

Dreaming was the main part of Mohave religion. Special talents, skills, and successes were believed to happen because of a person dreaming the right dreams. The ability to learn skills was not as important as being able to have great dreams.

This belief led natives to choose people for important tribal jobs such as chiefs, braves, shamans, singers, and funeral speakers, by the dreams they had dreamed. However, great dreams did not come easily. That is why those who truly did dream became leaders.

A club warriors used in a war.

It was thought that a dream a person might have had even before he or she was born would be remembered later in life.

Shamans were special religious "doctors" whose true dreams had made them powerful tribal members. Mainly shamans could, for instance, give feasts or take care of victory celebrations after wars.

Mohave shamans were also thought to cure a sick person or could say a special funeral oration. They did not learn from older doctors, but from birth learned only from their great Mastambo (leader) in dreams.

CLOTHING

The climate of a territory decided what kind of clothing villagers wore. The climate was usually so warm in Mohave territory that grown men needed only narrow breechclouts, and adult women wore simple aprons. On cool days, or in winter, both adults wore rabbitskin capes. Children did not need much clothing except during winter.

A Mohave hair ornament

Men's breechclouts were longer in the back than the front and were made from woven strands of willow tree innerbark.

Women had skirts that also were made of woven willow bark and went to the knees. When traveling, the women wore sandals woven of grass.

Women's hair was worn long and loose about the shoulders, with heavy bangs across their foreheads, like the men. Hair was very shiny because it was cleaned with a mixture of mud and boiled mesquite bark. Faces of both men and women were painted or tattooed. After white men arrived with beads to trade, the women wore beaded necklaces.

Men's hair was fixed as few other tribesmen's hair. They rolled their long hair into 20 or 30 rope-like strands which hung down the back, in what we would call curls. They also wore bangs.

Mohave man in breechclout

MESQUITE

Mesquite was so important to Mohave people that a special section on its uses, is needed. As in many desert tribes, Mohave people were known to call the bush their "tree of life." Fresh mesquite beans gave juice for the natives to drink. Ground-up bean pods made into a powder could be eaten as mush or baked into cakes.

The bark of mesquite was used for making shoes and clothing. Hair was dyed with mesquite juice. Roots of plants could be carved into musical instruments and into cradles; its sap made great glue. Even pottery was baked with mesquite fires.

The largest area of mesquite trees was used for building cremation fires in ancient days. Today Mohave territory has the largest stand of mesquite trees in California.

A mesquite plant

FOOD AND FARMING

Mohave people were very lucky to live on the banks of the Colorado River. Once a year, in the springtime, the river overflowed; then natives were able to grow corn, sunflowers, pumpkins, gourds, grasses such as panic grasses, and herbs on the desert flood plains.

These crops ripened quickly in the warm climate. It was important to raise enough plants to last until the next spring, but thankfully famines (times of no food) did not happen very often.

Mohave men did most of the land-clearing, as well as the planting and growing of their crops. Land-clearing meant breaking down the bushes growing on it and burning them. Only land not claimed by other tribespeople was free to be cultivated. Mohaves only claimed land they had cleared. Sometimes, the women helped with these jobs but mainly they harvested the crops.

Mohave basketry sieve for getting rid of the outside husks of wheat and other grains

To plant seeds, men used a stick cut into a wedge-shaped point. Then, holes about 4-6 inches deep and a foot apart were punched into the soft soil, but not in regular rows. The pattern of planting was usually long, curved, parallel rows.

Looking at the mounds of seed from an airplane today, gives a better picture of what the patterns were. They look something like ancient planting patterns of the country of Chile in South America. Those who study patterns feel the way of planting had to do with religious purification, as if the furrow lines are followed from the center of a line outward. Even today, the modern Mohaves will not reveal the meanings of these patterns.

Mohave women, following the men as they poked holes into the ground, dropped about six seeds into each hole, covered the seeds with soil and pressing down on the seeds to keep them in place.

Basketry burden basket for collecting food and carrying it home.

No fertilizer was used or needed because of silt, or top soil, in the flood water. However weeding was needed. For weeding the natives made sword-shaped wooden hoes.

There was one month of harvesting the crops that began in the middle of September. Corn was picked and the husking, meaning taking off the outside leaves, usually was done in the field.

Corn that was not eaten fresh or roasted, was completely dried in the sun on the roofs of the summer ramadas. Corn was then stored in large basketry granaries made from woven arrowwood branches with leaves still attached to them. Some people called these granaries giant bird nests.

In times of poor crops, women collected wild seeds in the bottom lands along the river, after floods had gone down. There were cactus fruit and desert plants growing in the surrounding land. Most important of the wild foods growing in their territory were the bean-like pods of the mesquite plant and what were called screwbeans.

Fish were important food. Natives caught them with seines, woven traps, dip nets, weirs, or by using small canoes. Mohave fishermen made canoe-shaped woven baskets to scoop fish from the water. They also caught fish with long-handled dip nets.

Weirs were brush fences with only one opening in them, built across smaller streams. A woven basket trap was put at the opening and fish were caught in the trap. A seine is an up and down (vertical) net with heavy rocks tied to one side, which trapped fish when the net was pulled together and brought into the boat. Men made very fine nets.

Liddell

A basketry scoop used to scoop fish from the water

Fish were usually eaten after they had been broiled on hot stone cones or boiled

A fiber line made from plant stem and tied to a cactus hook to catch fish

into a stew with corn, since Mohave fish were often not tasty. Mohaves often traded what deer they did kill for more, better-tasting fish. There was a taboo about eating the food they had caught or shot themselves.

Hunting was not needed as often as other tribes because the farming and gathering produced most of the Mohaves' foods. Since there was not much hunting, there were very few good, ancient hunting tools found. At times, rabbits were caught in snares or nets, or shot by small bows and arrows.

Sometimes small animals were knocked down with a throwing stick rather like a boomerang. Once in a while there was even a communal rabbit drive where a whole family would hold up nets and rabbits then would be scared into them.

TOOLS AND CRAFTS

Most tools were made just when needed, and then without care or decoration. Some archeologists believe the reason for no decorations on tools was because of funeral rituals, which meant the burning of all a person's belongings when he or she died. There was no handing down of items to relatives, so why bother with decorations?

For the same reason, baskets and pots were not well-made or decorated. There were not even stone or bone objects found by archeologists. What's more, scientists have found little, if any, woodworking. One reason possibly is that since their main food was grown for meals, not too many tools were needed.

TRADING

Mohave people believed in much trading, sometimes going as far west as the California coast to trade with the Gabrielinos for shells or soap-stone (soft stone) cooking ware they needed and enjoyed. The California Chumash and Yokut tribes joined in with the Mohave people when trading. In time of drought (no rain), wheat came in trade from the Quechan tribe.

Mohave became middle-men of East and West traders. They traded bas-kets, animal hides, salt, bows, dentalia and other shells that had been made into beads, acorns, and fish for things they, and others, might need.

A decorated gourd, possibly a trade item.

HISTORY

Around 1765, three years before the first Spanish Mission at San Diego was built, some Mohave men served as guides to help an early Spanish explorer, Francisco Garces, look around Southern California. It is interesting to note, however, no missions or Spanish settlements were ever built in Mohave territory.

In spite of many Spanish soldiers exploring what became California, Mohave people did not even try to change their own way of life until 1820, almost 50 years after trappers and fur traders from Europe began traveling through their land. Mohaves were fierce fighters against those trespassers who would tramp over farmlands.

The population of Mohaves before white people came is es-timated to have been a total of 20,000 people. After Euro-pean explorers arrived in the United States, the Mohave not only fought hard to keep their territory, but also against the diseases white people brought with them.

In fact, Mohaves suffered the loss of as many as 90% of their people to tuberculosis. Mohave people found that battles with sickness had made war too hard for them to win. The loss of so many villagers to tuberculosis, as well as to flu, pneumonia, and an eye disease called tracoma, which leads to blindness, were too great.

It had become a losing battle for Mohave people to fight not only other Native Americans, but also white settlers taking their land. In 1859, the Mohaves settled for permanent peace when they moved onto reservations built on their ancient territory.

Mohave men quickly learned the American settlers' kind of farming, ranching, and mining; but the people mainly became farmers, as they still are today. Farming is still important to both of their reservations.

A Mohave bowl

Mohave women did not work into white women's ways of living as easily as the men accepted change. However, some women became housekeepers at settlers' homes; handling jobs such as laundering clothes, taking care of children, shopping for women settlers, or making pottery, beading, and other ornaments.

Shawl decorated with beads received from an explorer.

Today's Mohaves are no longer war-like people. In the river area these days, they still grow cotton, alfalfa, melons, and lettuce as the main crops. Villagers now use irrigation to water their plants.

In 1942 a large group of Japanese people, who were sent to Mohave reservation land during World War II, organized Mohave farming. As a result, in 1976 Fort Mohave people finally earned enough money to pay for their own irrigation system.

Mohaves also have made money from the leasing of land to non-Mohave people. In 1995 fifteen thousand acres were being rented to others, while the Mohave reservation's Tribal Coop still farms 130,000 acres of their own land.

Today, casinos built on their land bring in from eight to ten million dollars a year to the tribe. This means the people have been able to add to scholarships for young Mohave students studying tribal history and Native American culture.

Ancient Mohave trading paths first became the property of the United States Corps of Army Engineers, but finally are now large parts of Interstate Highway 40 and of the Santa Fé Railroad.

These days, natives live in two groups, Fort Mohave Indian Reservation and Colorado River Reservation. The reservations have separate problems and tribal councils. Both have city and criminal courts.

Chemehuevis (chem ee whuay vees), Hopis (Hope ees) and Navahoes, as well as Mohaves, stay at the larger Colorado River Reservation these days, while others live north, at the smaller Fort Mohave. According to some sociologists, in 1995 there was a total of 2,900 people living on both reservations. One source says more than one-half of the natives speak their ancient language in reservation homes today. Other scientists say only those Mohaves over the age of 30 still speak their language.

But all Mohaves feel that Indians can never stop being Native Americans. They still respect Mother Earth and the older generations around them, still cherish their children, and treat each other well.

A Mohave man with a bone as decoration in his nose, his hair tightly rolled into curls.

MOHAVE OUTLINE

I. Introduction
   A. Where the name came from
   B. Where the tribe lived
   C. Importance of Colorado River
   D. Ancient population
   E Description of Mohave natives
   F. Emotions of people
   G. Curiosity of natives
   H. Mohave occupations
   I. War!
      1. War weapons
      2. Reasons for war
   J. Scattered settlements

II. Territory, Village Sites, Homes
   A. Three areas
   B. Where bands lived
   C. Rancherias
   D. Climate
   E. Plants
      1. Flooding
         a. Planting of corn, beans, pumpkin, and melons
      2. Hunting, gathering, and fishing
   F. Winter home description
   G. C-shaped homes
   H. Ramadas

III. Village Life
   A. Using the river and pots
   B. Chief and subchiefs
      1. Kind of power and ruling
   C. Customs
      1. Marriage and public ceremonies
   D. Entertainment

IV. Life cycle
   A. Baby birth
      1. Happy childhood
      2. Sickness and shaman
   B. Death customs

V. Religion
- A. Importance of dreams
- B. Important tribal leaders and dreams
- C. Shamans' jobs

VI. Clothing
- A. Kinds of clothing
    1. Men, women, and children
    2. Hair styles and care
- B. Tatooes
- C. Ornaments

VII. Mesquite
- A. Uses

VIII. Food and farming
- A. Men's jobs
- B. Women's jobs
- C. Patterns of planting
- D. Harvest month
- E. Ways of eating corn
- F. Ways of catching fish
    1. Ways of cooking or preserving fish
- G . Cooking and other tools

IX. Trading
- A. Mohave partners for trading and why
- B. Tell of middlemen trading

X. History
- A. Guiding for Spanish explorer
- B. Did not change ways until when
- C. Ancient population of Mohaves
- D. Sickness and dying
- E. 1859 and permanent peace
- F. Working for whites
- G. Japanese helping farming
- H. Today
    1. Scholarships for students
    2. The two reservations were?
    3. New population
    4. They respect, today?

NATIVE AMERICAN WORDS WE KNOW AND USE

PLANTS AND TREES

hickory
pecan
yucca
mesquite
saguaro

ANIMALS

caribou
chipmunk
cougar
jaguar
opossum
moose

STATES

Dakota – friend
Ohio – good river
Minnesota – waters that
   reflect the sky
Oregon – beautiful water
Nebraska – flat water
Arizona
Texas

FOODS

avocado
hominy
maize (corn)
persimmon
tapioca
succotash

GEOGRAPHY

bayou – marshy body of water
savannah – grassy plain
pasadena – valley

WEATHER

blizzard
Chinook (warm, dry wind)

FURNITURE

hammock

HOUSE

wigwam
wickiup
tepee
igloo

INVENTIONS

toboggan

BOATS

canoe
kayak

OTHER WORDS

caucus – group meeting
mugwump – loner politician
squaw – woman
papoose – baby

CLOTHING

moccasin
parka
mukluk – slipper
poncho

MOHAVE BIBLIOGRAPHY

Goodchild, Peter. *Survival Skills of the North American Indians.* Chicago, Il: Chicago Review Press, 1984.

Heizer, Robert F. , volume editor. *Handbook of North American Indians, volume 8.* Washington, D.C.: Smithsonian Institution, 1978.

Nabokov, Peter, and Easton, Robert. *Native American Architecture.* New York, N.Y.: Oxford University Press, Inc., 1989.

Ortiz, Alfonso, volume editor. *Handbook of North American Indians, volume 10.* Washington, D.C: Smithsonian Institution, 1983.

Sturtivant, William C., technical consultant and Talor, Colin F, Editorial consultant. *The Native Americans.* New York City, N.Y.: Smithmark, reprinted 1991.

The Reader's Digest, Maxwell, James A., Senior editor. *America's Fascinating Indian Heritage.* Pleasantville, N.Y.: c 1978.

Tunis, Edward. *Indians.* Cleveland and New York, N.Y.: The World Publishing Company, 1959.

Waldman, Carl. *Atlas of the North American Indian.* New York City, N.Y. : Facts on File, Inc. , 1985.

Yellow Robe, Rosebud. *An Album of the American Indians.* New York, N.Y.: Franklin Watts, Inc., 1969.

GENERAL BIBLIOGRAPHY

Billard, Jules B., ed. *The World of the American Indian.* Washington, D.C.: National Geographic Society, 1989.

Demallie, Raymond, and Ortiz, Alfonso. *North American Indian Anthology.* Norman, OK and London: University of OK Press, 1994.

Josephy, Alvin M., Jr.. *500 Nations.* (A Borzoi Book). New York, NY: Alfred A. Knopf, Inc. , 1994.

Josephy, Alvin M., Jr.. *The Indian Heritage of America.* Boston: Houghton Mifflin, 1991.

Klein, Barry T.. *Reference Encyclopedia of the American Indian.* Nyack, NY: Todd Publications, 1998.

Lobb, Allen. *Indian Baskets of the Pacific Northwest and Alaska.* Portland, OR: Graphic Arts Center Publishing Co., 1990.

Maxwell, James A.. *America's Fascinating Indian Heritage.* Pleasantville, NY and Montreal: The Reader's Digest Association, Inc., 1978.

Milner, Clyde A., and O'Connor, Carol A.,II.. *The Oxford History of the American West.* New York and Oxford: Oxford University Press, 1994.

Sturtevant, William C. and Taylor, Colin F., consultants. *The Native Americans.* New York: Smithmark Publishers, (Salamander Books), 1992.

Thomas, D. H.; Miller, Jay; White, Richard; Nabokov, Peter; and Deloria, Philip J.. *The Native Americans.* Atlanta: Turner Publications, 1993.

GENERAL BIBLIOGRAPHY (continued)

The Editors of Time-Life Books. *The First Americans*. Alexandria, VA: Time-Life Books, 1992.

Tunis, Edwin. *Indians*. Cleveland, Ohio and New York, NY: The World Publications Co., 1959.

Turnbaugh, S. P. and William A.. *Indian Baskets*. Westchester, PA: Schiffer Publishers, Ltd., 1986.

Weatherford, Jack. *Native Roots*. New York, NY: Crown Publishers, 1991.

Credits:
Pollard Group, Inc., Tacoma, Washington 98409
Dona McAdam, Mac on the Hill, Seattle, Washington 98109

Special thanks:
Mary Basta for her artwork on page 38.